A Violin Advent

25 Days of Christmas Solos and Duets for a Most Joyous Season

Book One

Myanna Harvey and Cassia Harvey

Cover Image
The Miriam and Ira D. Wallach Division of Art, Prints and Photographs: Picture Collection, The New York Public Library. "Christmas greetings." The New York Public Library Digital Collections. https://digitalcollections.nypl.org/items/510d47e3-6f8c-a3d9-e040-e00a18064a99

CHP431

©2022 C. Harvey Publications®
All Rights Reserved.
www.charveypublications.com - print books
www.learnstrings.com - downloadable books
www.harveystringarrangements.com - chamber music

Table of Contents

                                                    Page

	Page
How the Book Works	3
Dec. 1: The First Noel	4
Dec. 2: We Three Kings	6
Dec. 3: Good King Wenceslas	8
Dec. 4: Go, Tell It on the Mountain	10
Dec. 5: Jingle Bells	12
Dec. 6: O Come, All Ye Faithful	16
Dec. 7: Away in a Manger	18
Dec. 8: O Christmas Tree	20
Dec. 9: Angels We Have Heard on High	22
Dec. 10: Up on the Housetop	26
Dec. 11: God Rest Ye, Merry Gentlemen	28
Dec. 12: O Little Town of Bethlehem	30
Dec. 13: I Saw Three Ships	32
Dec. 14: March from **The Nutcracker**	34
Dec. 15: What Child is This	38
Dec. 16: O Holy Night	42
Dec. 17: O Come, O Come Emmanuel	46
Dec. 18: The Twelve Days of Christmas	48
Dec. 19: Carol of the Bells	52
Dec. 20: Deck the Halls	54
Dec. 21: Hark, the Herald Angels Sing	56
Dec. 22: Waltz from **The Nutcracker**	58
Dec. 23: Joy to the World	62
Dec. 24: Silent Night	64
Dec. 25: We Wish You a Merry Christmas	66

How the Book Works

This book can work as a music advent calendar, giving you warm-up exercises, melodies, and variations on carols to play on the days leading up to Christmas.

On each day of December, you can play a warm-up, then the melody, and finally work on the variation. Then, you can play the melodies and variations with violin duet parts at a lesson or a chamber music session.

Looking to play Christmas music with friends? This book is compatible with the Viola and the Cello books and can be used to play Christmas duets with those instruments as well!

Play-Along Files

Links to available play-along files and videos can be found at www.charveypublications.com/adventplayalong.

Performance Suggestion

When performing from the book, a good way to format a carol would be to play the Melody, the Variation, and then the Melody again.

Please note: Playing the Melody simultaneously with another player playing the Variation is not recommended.

Free Sheet Music from C. Harvey Publications!

Free exercises, solos, and duets can be found on our blog at
https://www.charveypublications.com/better-string-playing-blog

Have a Question?

We are here to answer questions about the book! Email us at charveypublications@gmail.com or fill out the contact form here:
https://www.charveypublications.com/contact.html

©2022 C. Harvey Publications® All Rights Reserved.

December 1st: Warm-Up for The First Noel

C. Harvey

December 1st Melody: The First Noel

Traditional French Carol

©2022 C. Harvey Publications All Rights Reserved.

December 1st Variation: The First Noel

M. Harvey, after Traditional Melody

December 1st Duet Part: The First Noel

M. Harvey

©2022 C. Harvey Publications All Rights Reserved.

December 2nd: Warm-Up for We Three Kings

C. Harvey

Tremolo: In the upper half of the bow, move the bow back and forth very lightly, and as fast as possible for the length of the note.

December 2nd Melody: We Three Kings

J. Hopkins

Moderato

December 4th: Warm-Up for Go, Tell It On the Mountain

C. Harvey

December 4th Melody: Go, Tell It On the Mountain

Traditional African-American Spiritual

December 5th: Warm-Ups for Jingle Bells

G Major Scale

C. Harvey

G Major Etude

C. Harvey

©2022 C. Harvey Publications All Rights Reserved.

Agility Etude

C. Harvey

December 5th Melody: Jingle Bells

Allegro

J. Pierpont

December 5th Variation: Jingle Bells

Allegro

M. Harvey, after J. Pierpont

©2022 C. Harvey Publications All Rights Reserved.

A Violin Advent, Book One

15

December 5th Duet Part: Jingle Bells

M. Harvey

©2022 C. Harvey Publications All Rights Reserved.

December 6th: Warm-Up for O Come, All Ye Faithful

C. Harvey

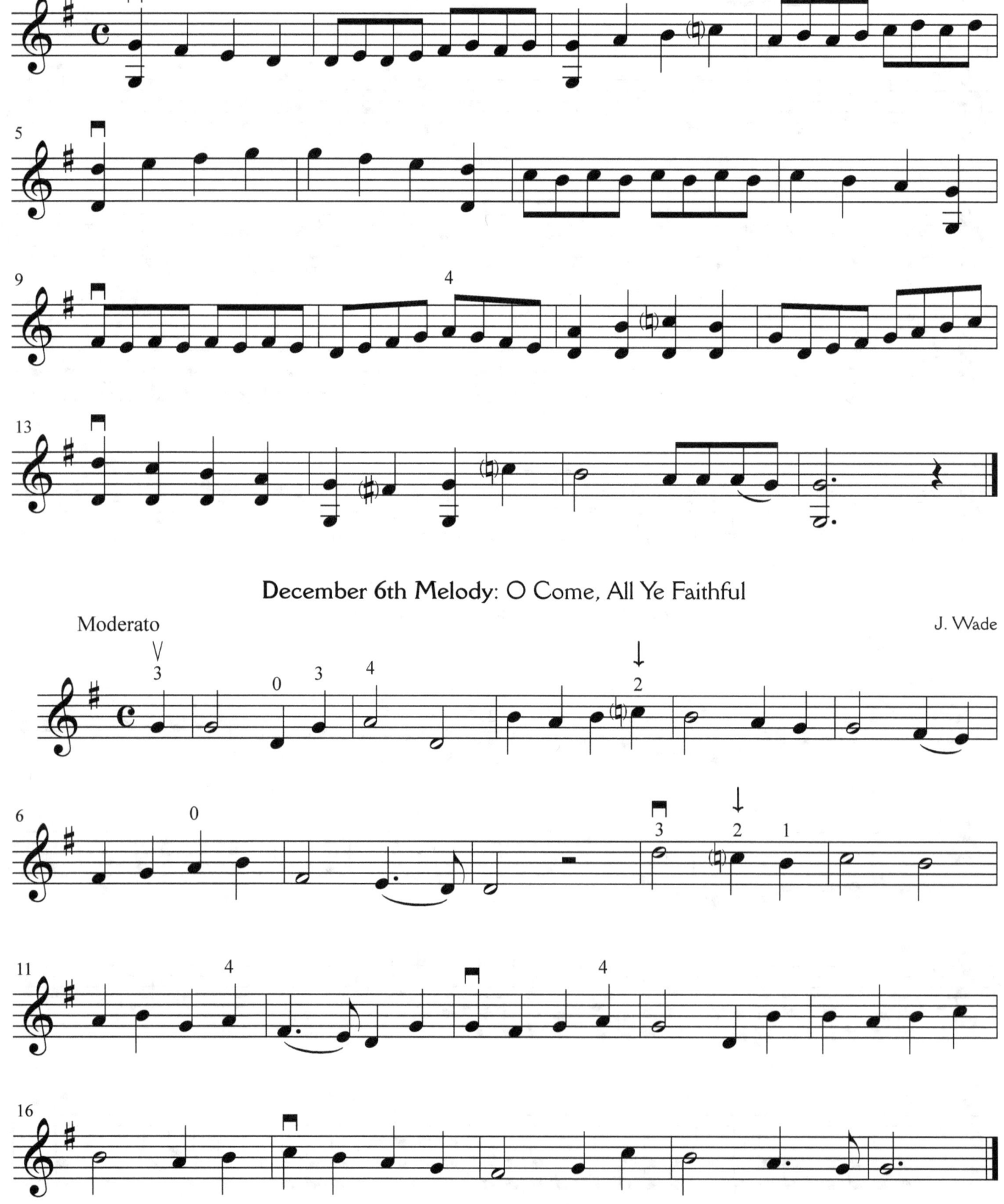

December 6th Melody: O Come, All Ye Faithful

J. Wade

©2022 C. Harvey Publications All Rights Reserved.

A Violin Advent, Book One

December 6th Variation: O Come, All Ye Faithful

M. Harvey, after J. Wade

December 6th Duet Part: O Come, All Ye Faithful

M. Harvey

©2022 C. Harvey Publications All Rights Reserved.

December 7th: Warm-Up for Away in a Manger

C. Harvey

December 7th Melody: Away in a Manger

J. Murray

©2022 C. Harvey Publications All Rights Reserved.

December 7th Variation: Away in a Manger

M. Harvey, after J. Murray

Andante

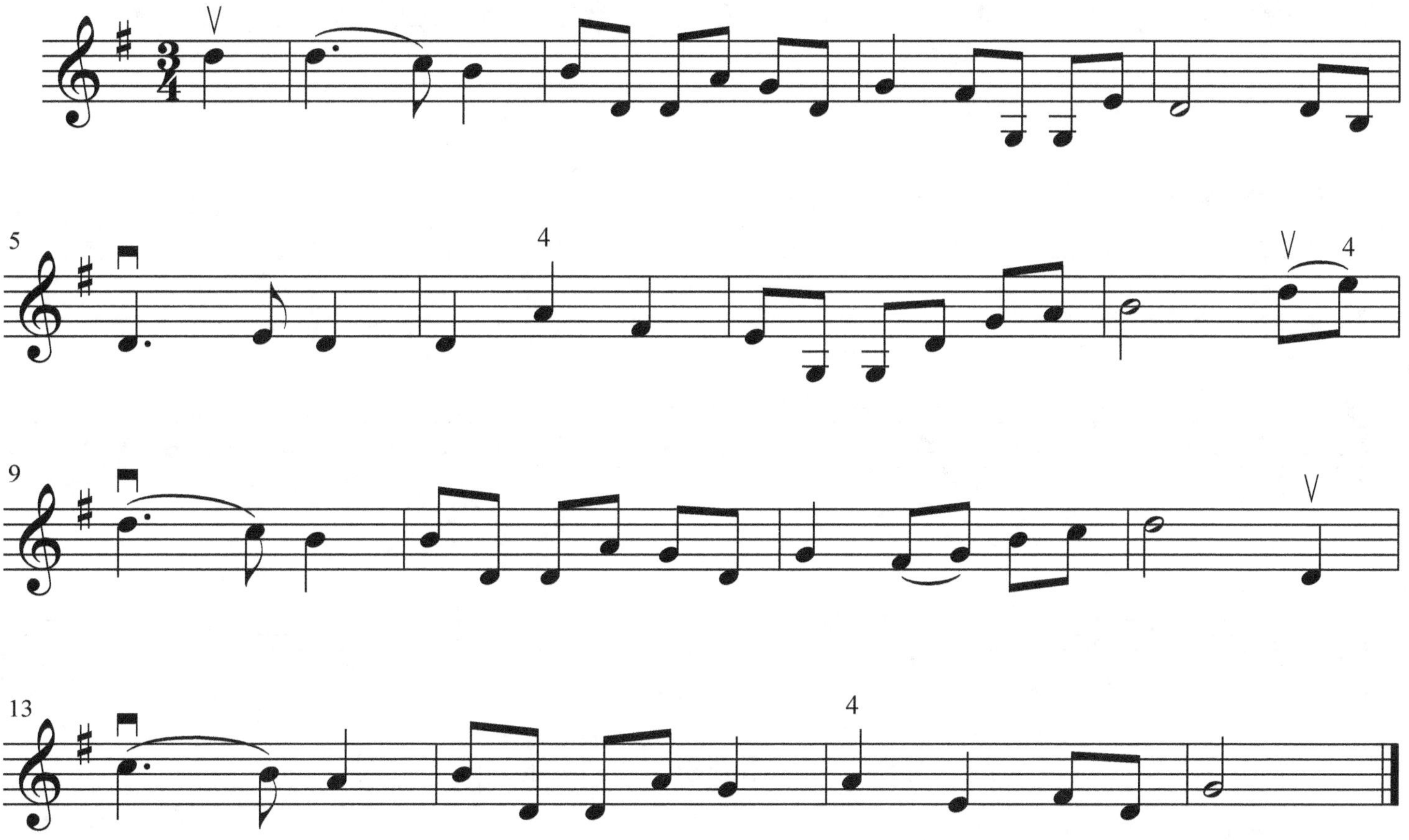

December 7th Duet Part: Away in a Manger

M. Harvey

Andante

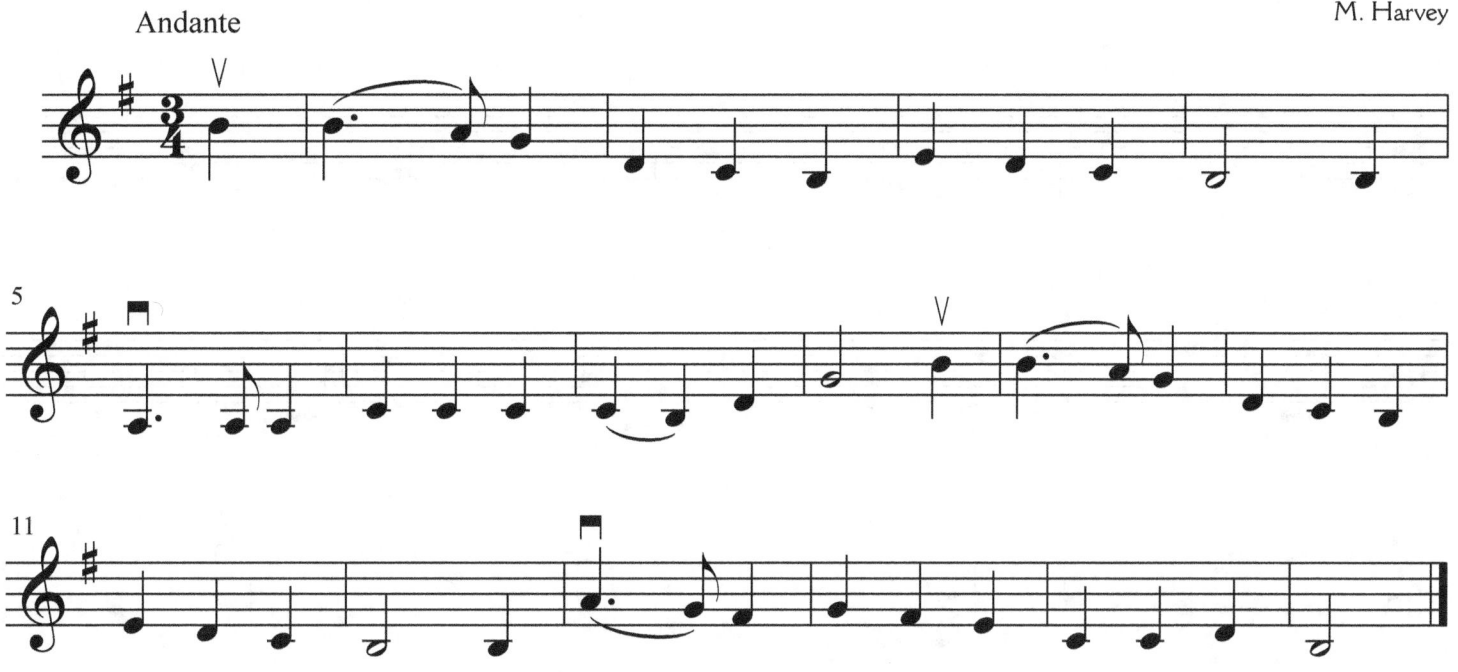

December 8th: Warm-Up for O Christmas Tree

C. Harvey

December 8th Melody: O Christmas Tree

Traditional Melody

Moderato

December 8th Variation: O Christmas Tree

December 8th Duet Part: O Christmas Tree

December 9th: Warm-Ups for Angels We Have Heard on High

C. Harvey

D Major Scale Etude

Mordent

is played

String Crossing Etude

C. Harvey

December 9th Melody: Angels We Have Heard on High

Traditional Melody

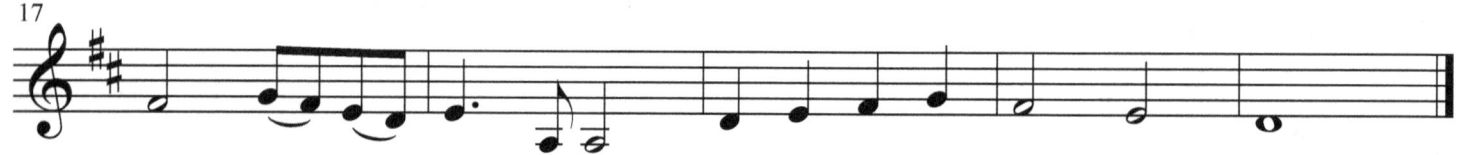

December 9th Variation: Angels We Have Heard on High

M. Harvey, after Trad. Melody

December 9th Duet Part: Angels We Have Heard on High

M. Harvey

Allegro

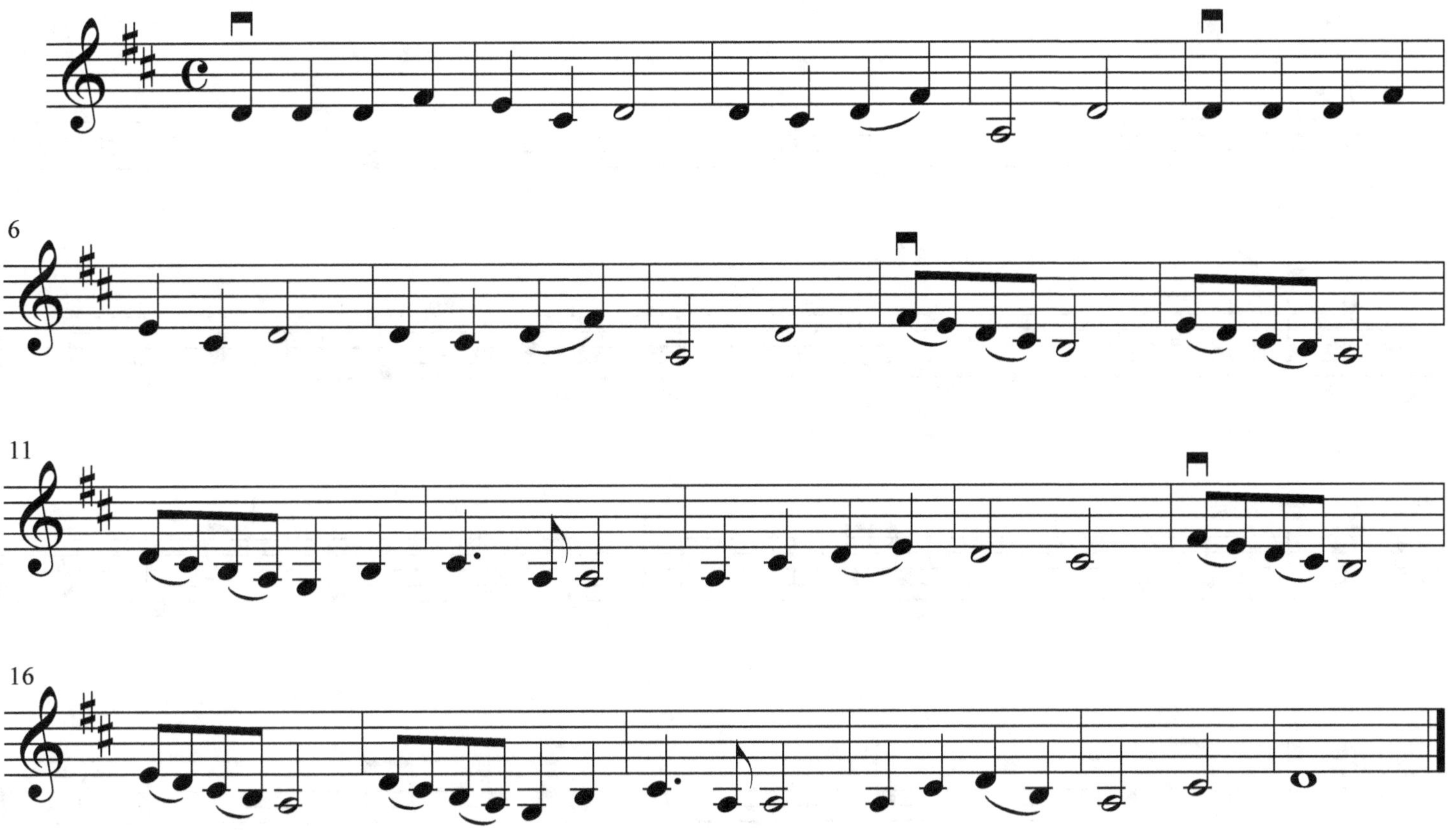

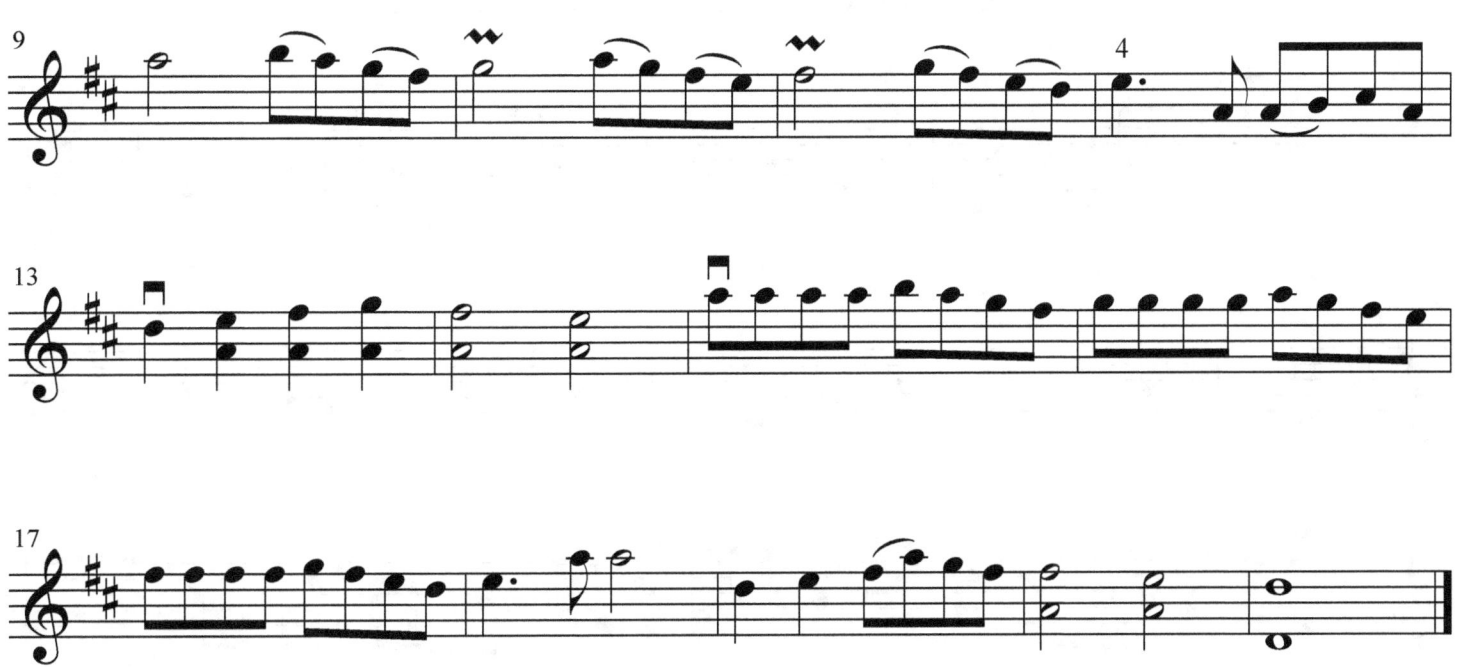

December 10th: Warm-Up for Up on the Housetop

C. Harvey

Left-hand pizzicato

December 10th Melody: Up on the Housetop

B. Hanby

Allegro

©2022 C. Harvey Publications All Rights Reserved.

December 10th Variation: Up on the Housetop

M. Harvey, after B. Hanby

December 10th Duet Part: Up on the Housetop

M. Harvey

©2022 C. Harvey Publications All Rights Reserved.

December 11th: Warm-Up for God Rest Ye, Merry Gentlemen

C. Harvey

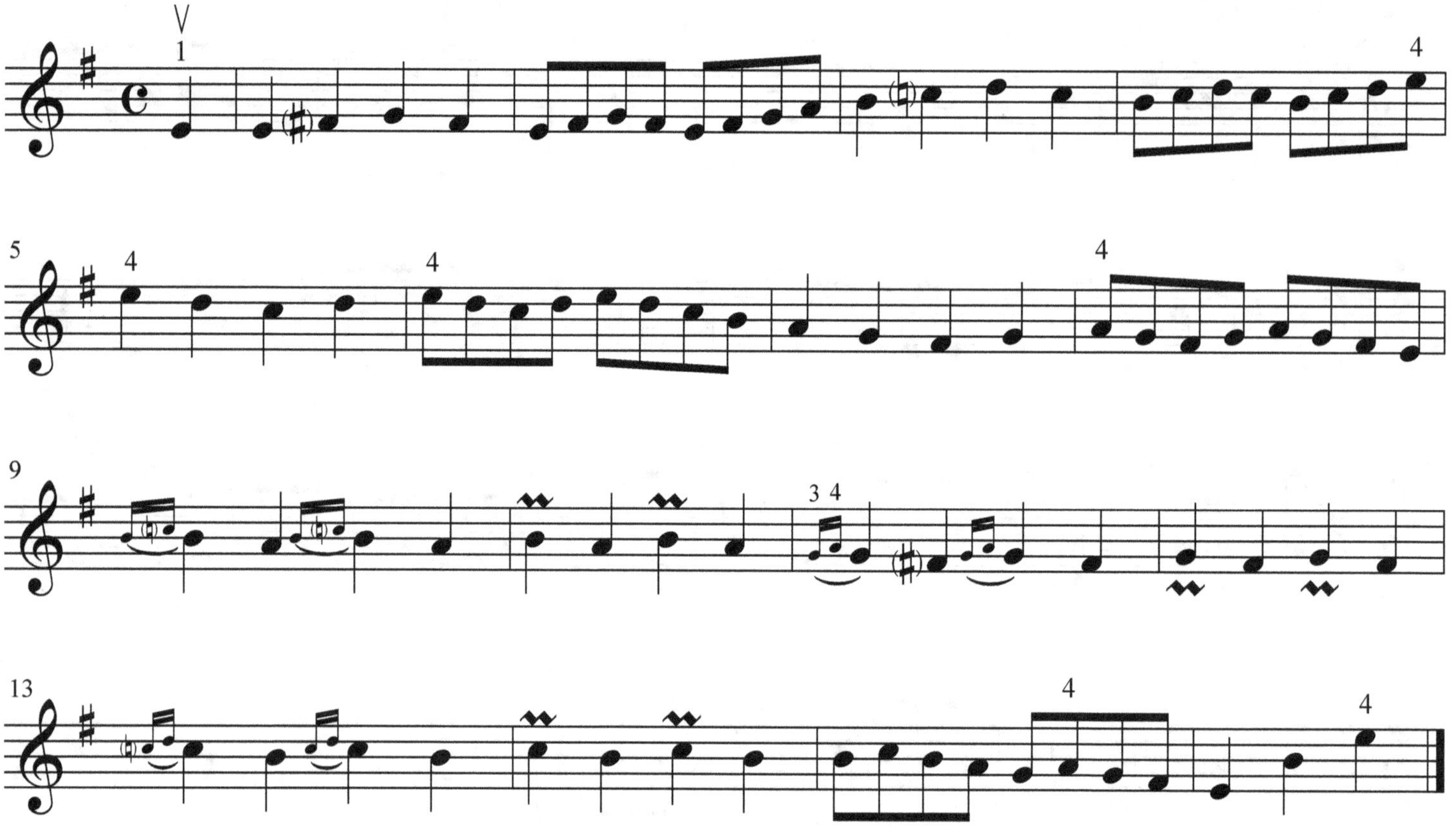

December 11th Melody: God Rest Ye, Merry Gentlemen

Moderato

Traditional Melody

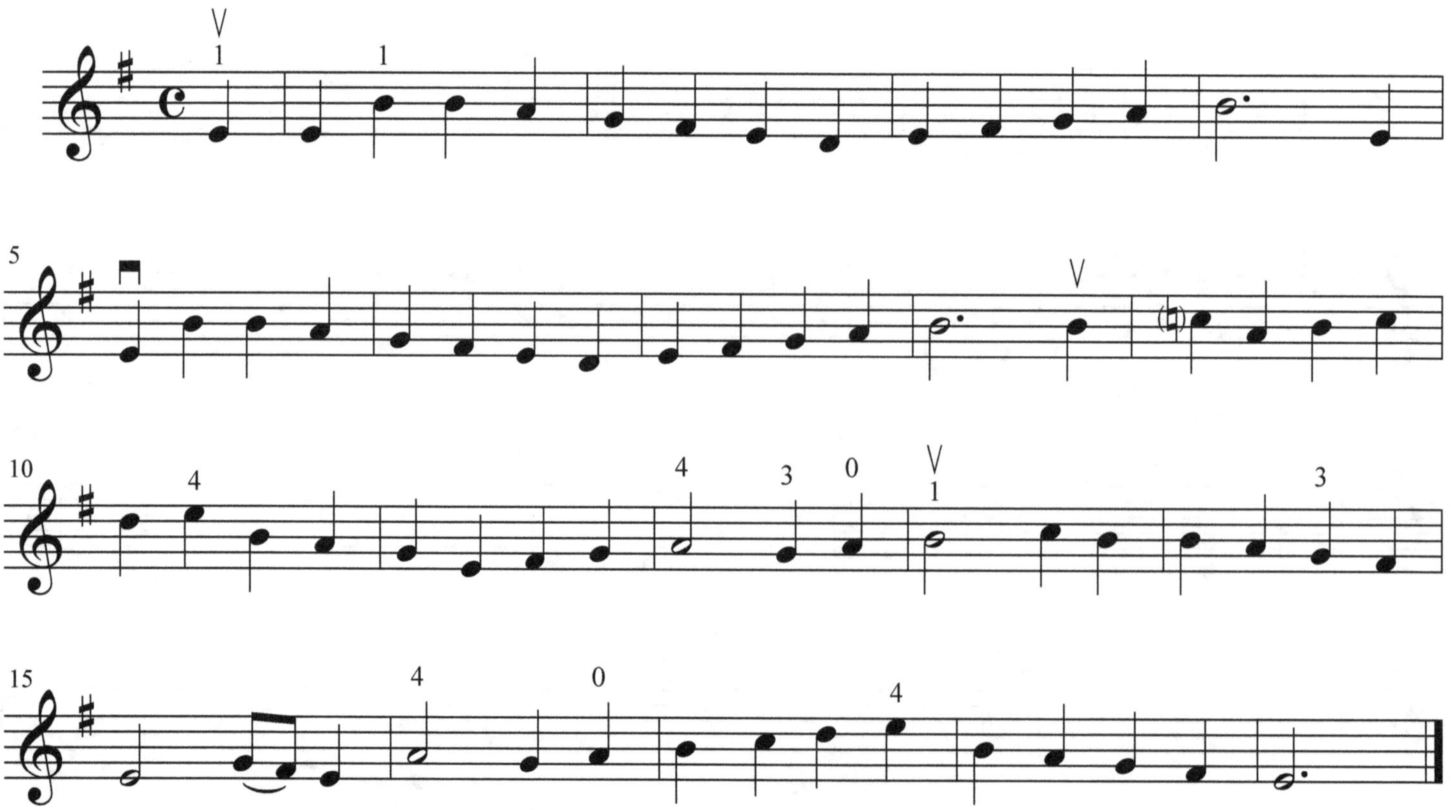

December 12th: Warm-Up for O Little Town of Bethlehem

C. Harvey

December 12th Melody: O Little Town of Bethlehem

Andante

L. Redner

A Violin Advent, Book One

December 12th Variation: O Little Town of Bethlehem

M. Harvey, after L. Redner

Andante

December 12th Duet Part: O Little Town of Bethlehem

M. Harvey

Andante

©2022 C. Harvey Publications All Rights Reserved.

December 13th: Warm-Up for I Saw Three Ships

C. Harvey

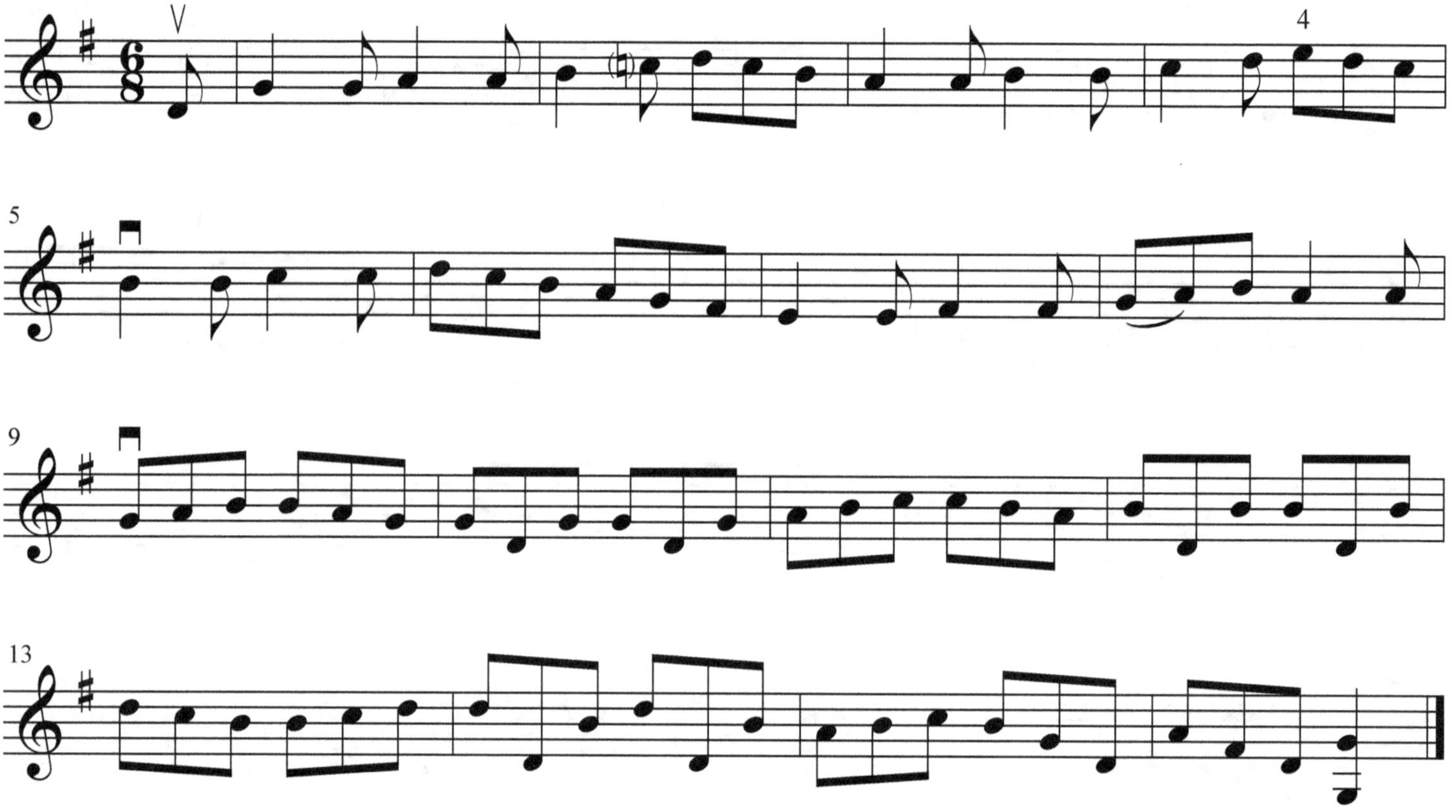

December 13th Melody: I Saw Three Ships

Traditional Melody

Vivace

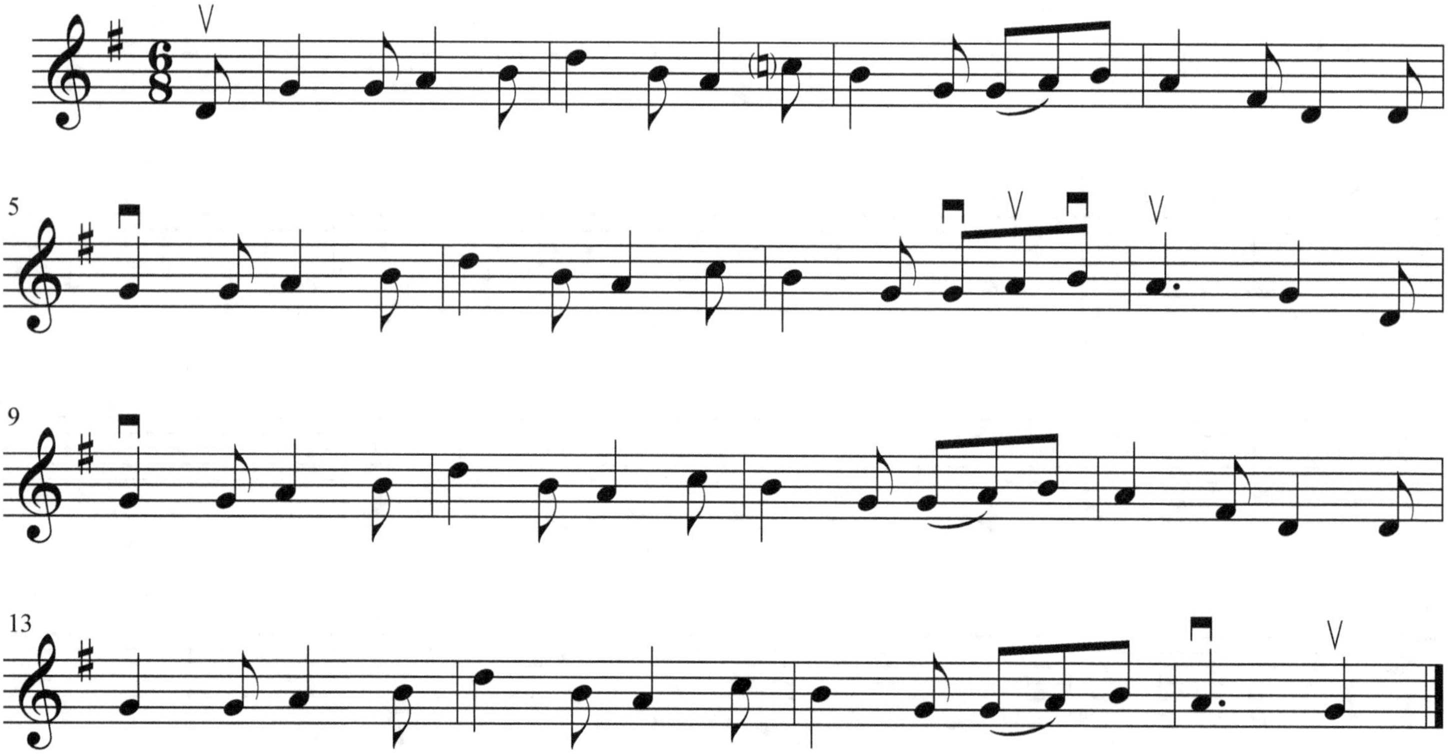

A Violin Advent, Book One

December 13th Variation: I Saw Three Ships

M. Harvey, after Traditional Melody

December 13th Duet Part: I Saw Three Ships

M. Harvey

©2022 C. Harvey Publications All Rights Reserved.

December 14th: Warm-Ups for March from *The Nutcracker*

D Major Scale Rhythm No. 1

C. Harvey

D Major Scale Rhythm No. 2

C. Harvey

D Major Rhythm Etude

C. Harvey

C# and A#

C. Harvey

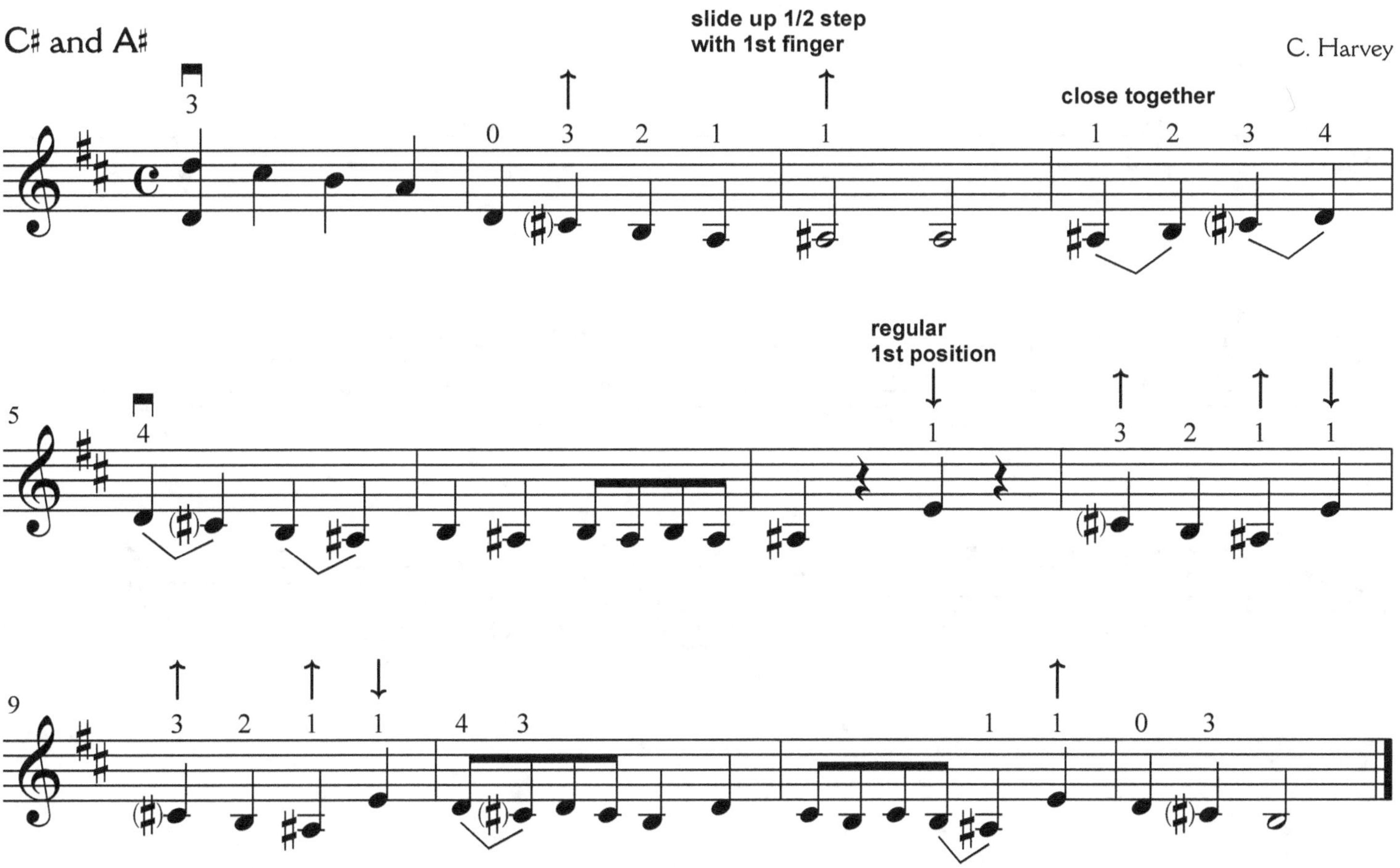

slide up 1/2 step with 1st finger

close together

regular 1st position

December 14th Melody: March from *The Nutcracker*

P. Tchaikovsky

Tempo di Marcia

A Violin Advent, Book One

December 14th Variation: March from *The Nutcracker*

Tempo di Marcia

P. Tchaikovsky, arr. M. Harvey

December 14th Duet Part: March from *The Nutcracker*

M. Harvey, after P. Tchaikovsky

Tempo di Marcia

©2022 C. Harvey Publications All Rights Reserved.

December 15th: Warm-Ups for What Child Is This

C. Harvey

D Minor Etude No. 1

D Minor Etude No. 2

C. Harvey

December 15th Melody: What Child Is This

Moderato

Traditional Melody

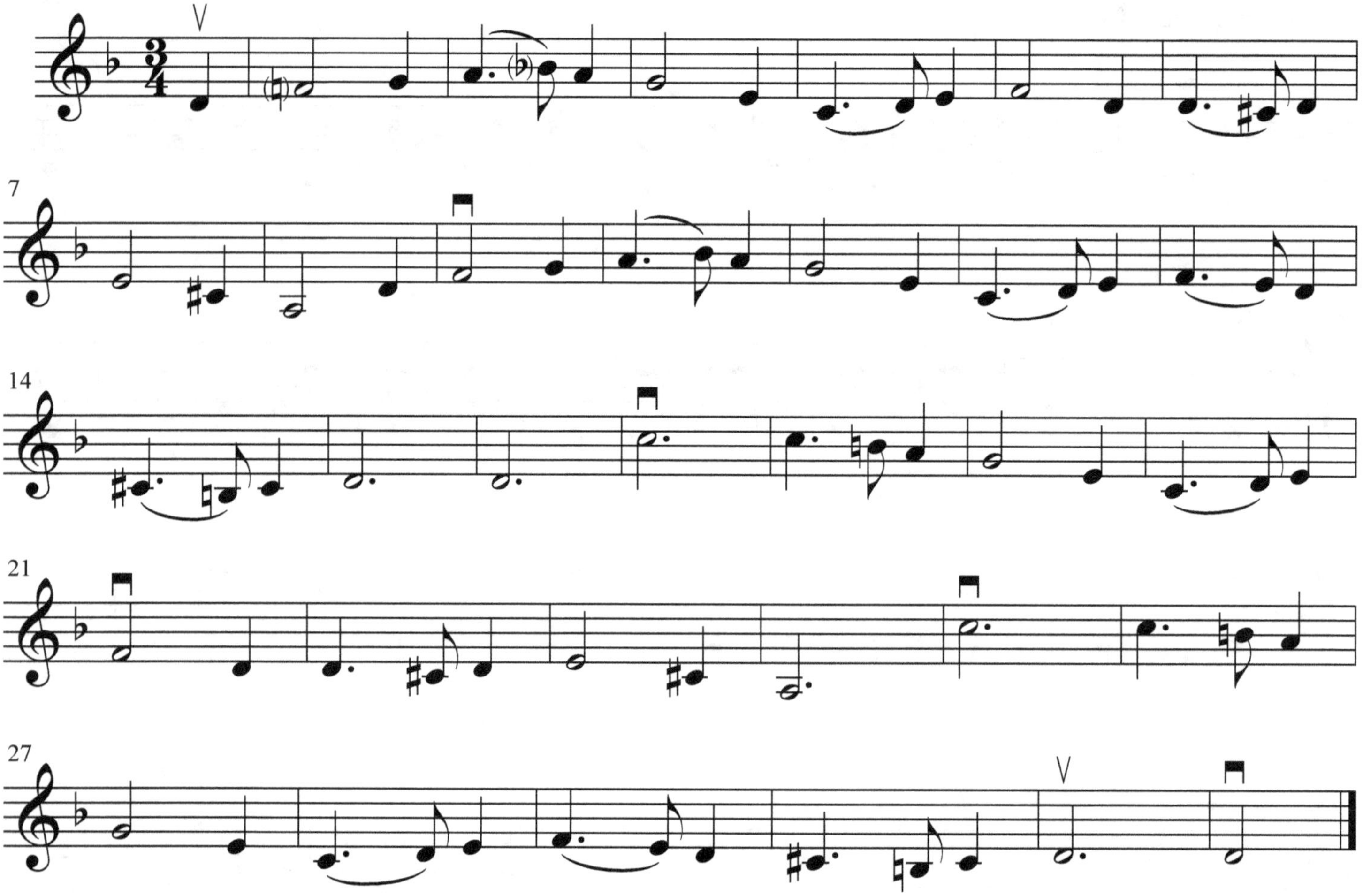

December 15th Variation: What Child Is This

Moderato

M. Harvey, after Traditional Melody

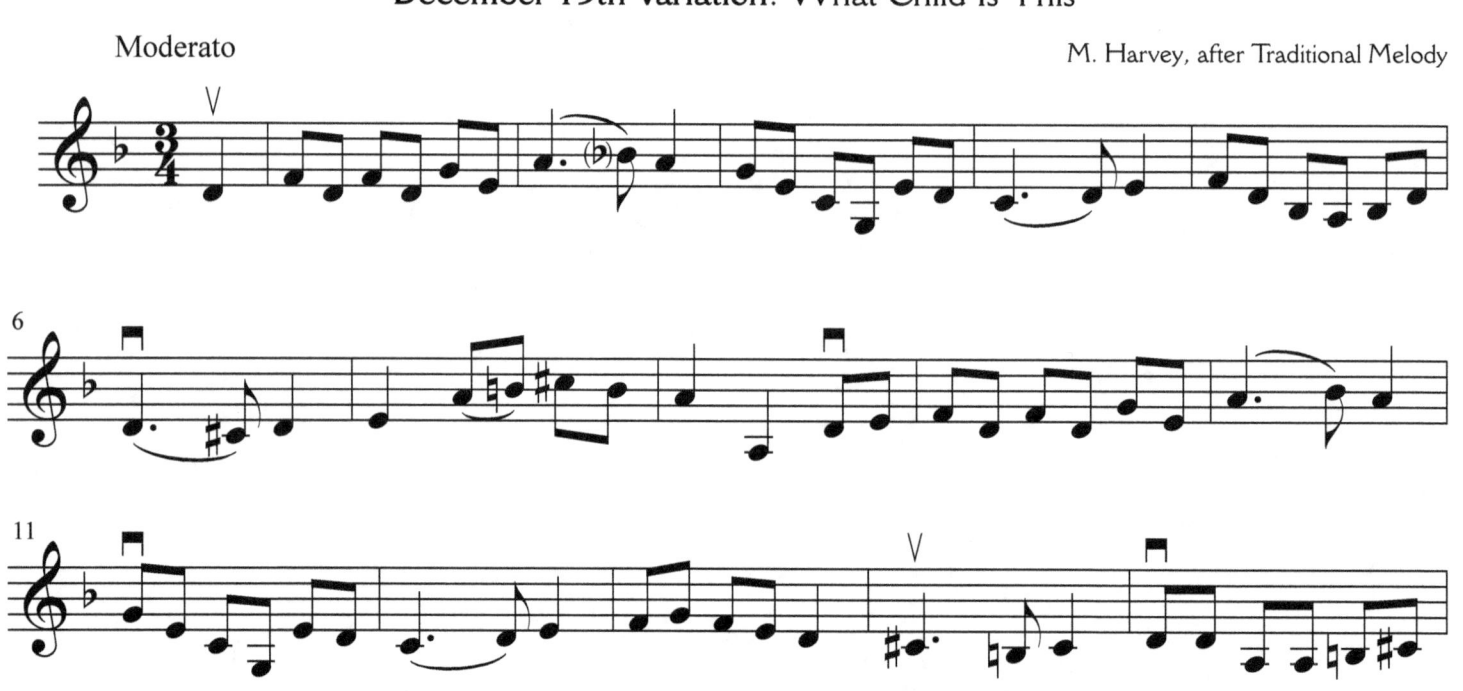

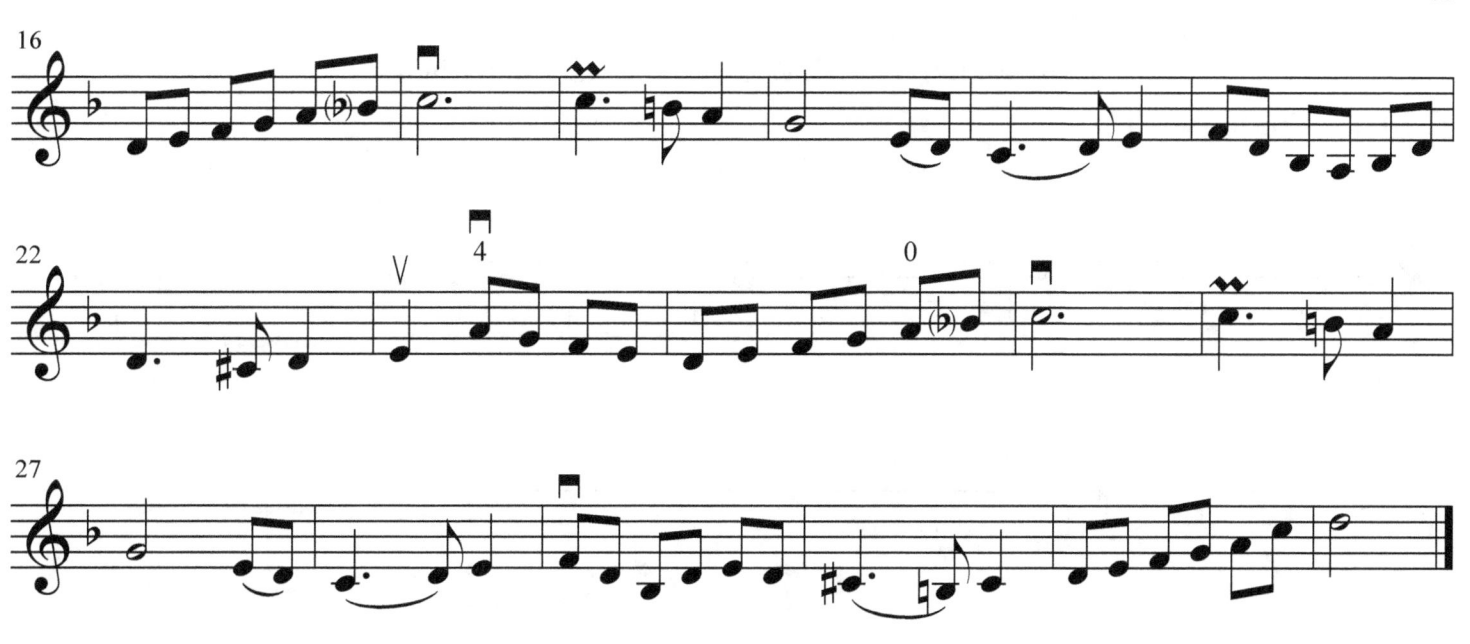

December 15th Duet Part: What Child Is This

M. Harvey

Moderato

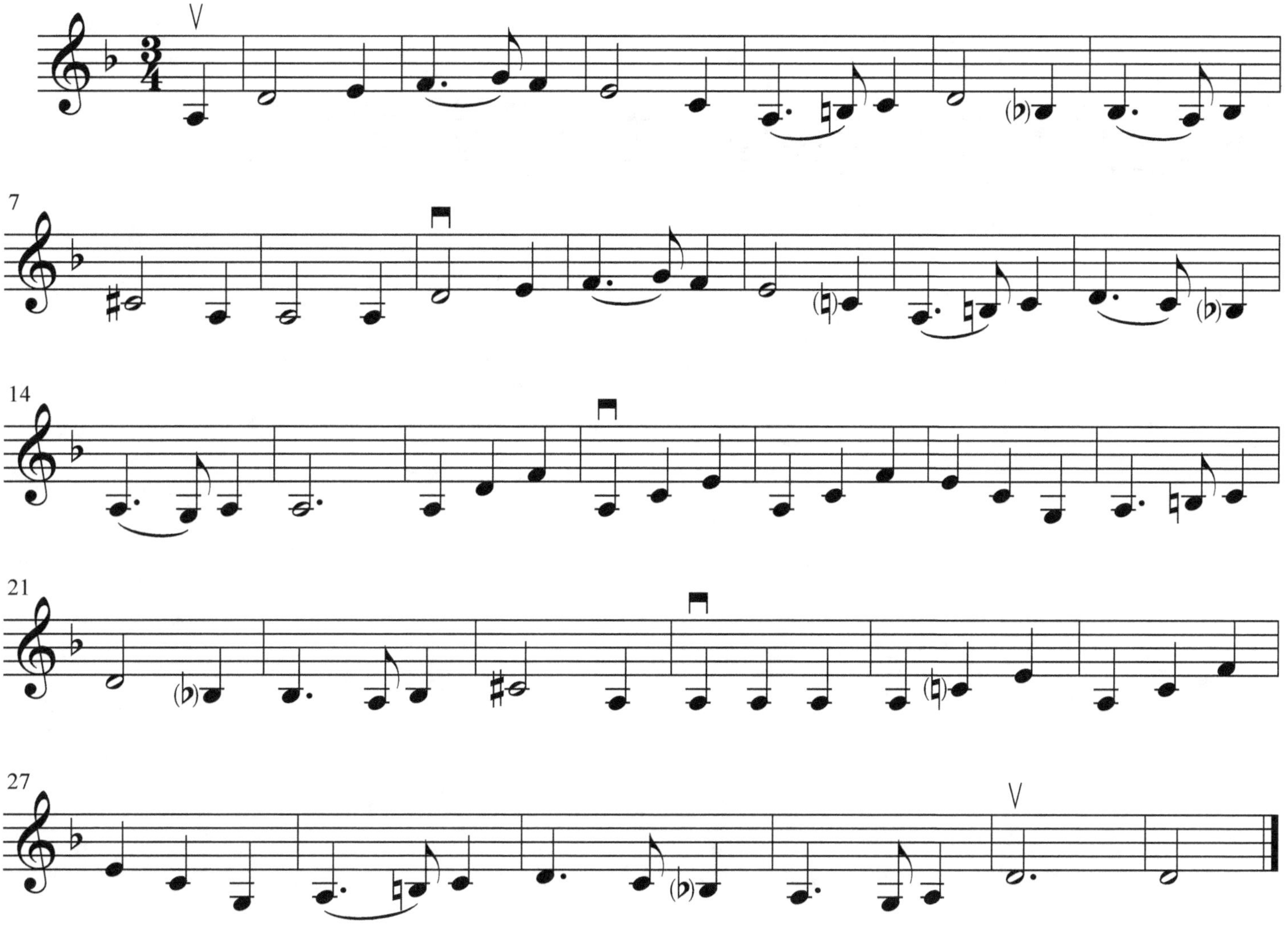

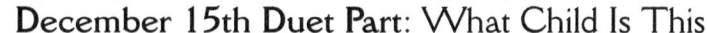

December 16th: Warm-Ups for O Holy Night

C Major Etude No. 1

C. Harvey

C Major Etude No. 2

C. Harvey

December 16th Melody: O Holy Night

Andante

A. Adam

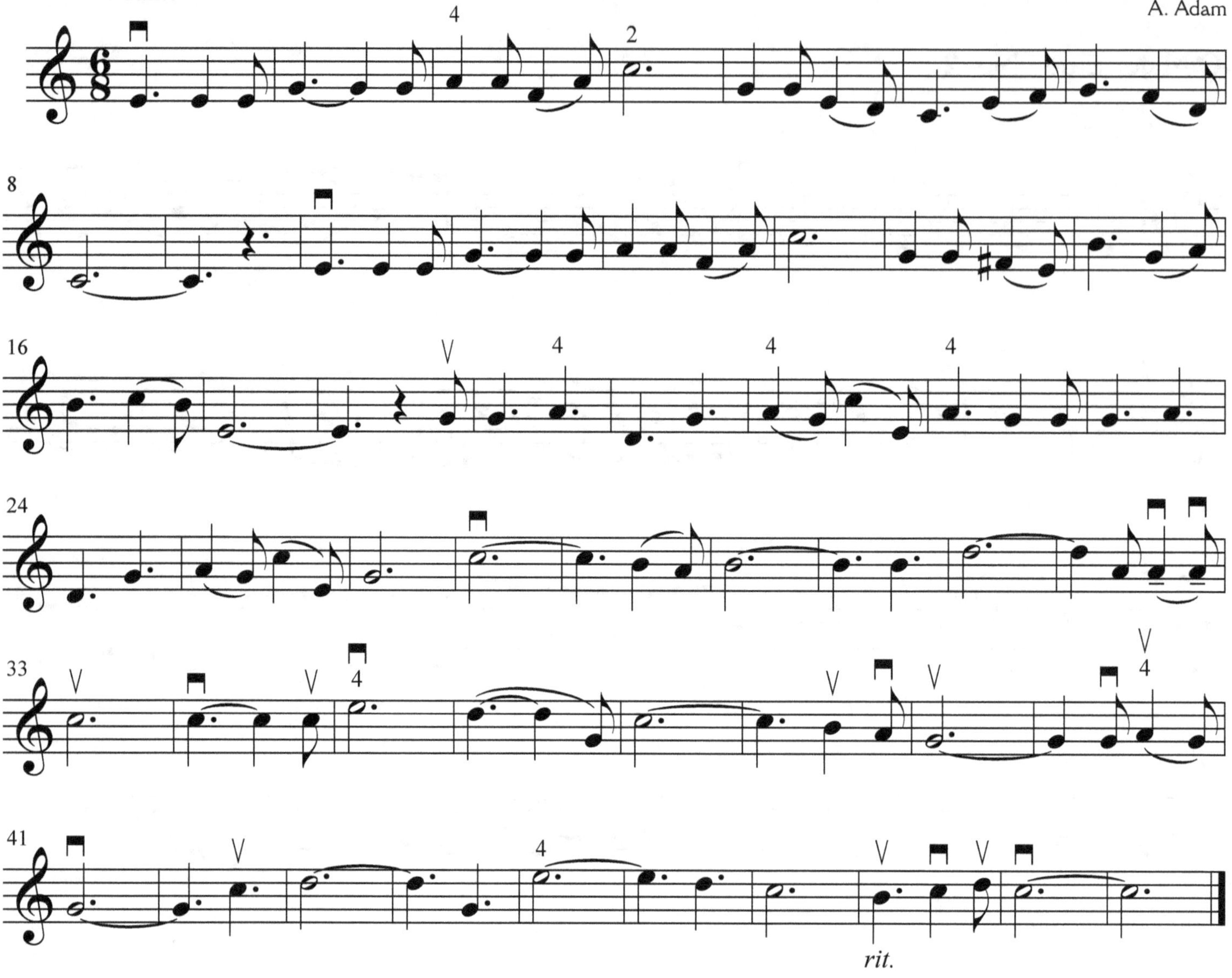

December 16th Variation: O Holy Night

Andante

M. Harvey, after A. Adam

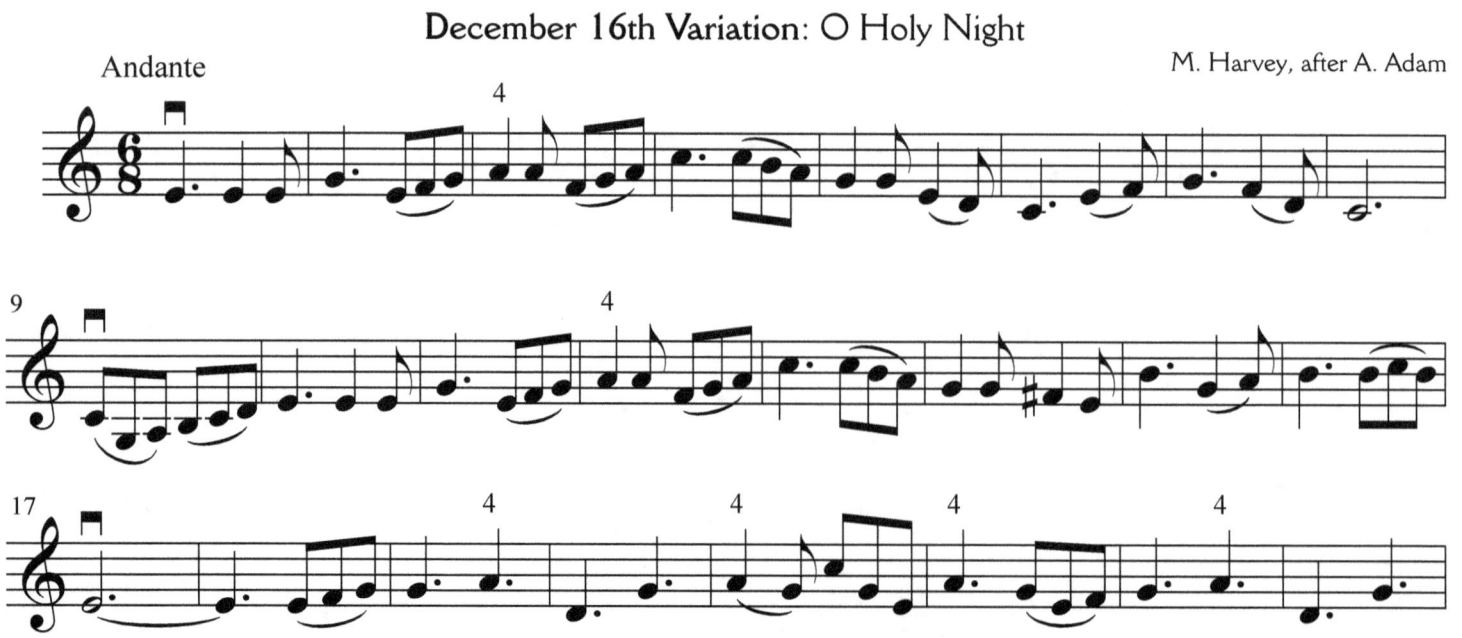

A Violin Advent, Book One 45

December 16th Duet Part: O Holy Night

M. Harvey

December 17th: Warm-Up for O Come, O Come Emmanuel

C. Harvey

December 17th Melody: O Come, O Come Emmanuel

Plainsong

©2022 C. Harvey Publications All Rights Reserved.

December 17th Variation: O Come, O Come Emmanuel

Andante

M. Harvey, after Plainsong

December 17th Duet Part: O Come, O Come Emmanuel

M. Harvey

Andante

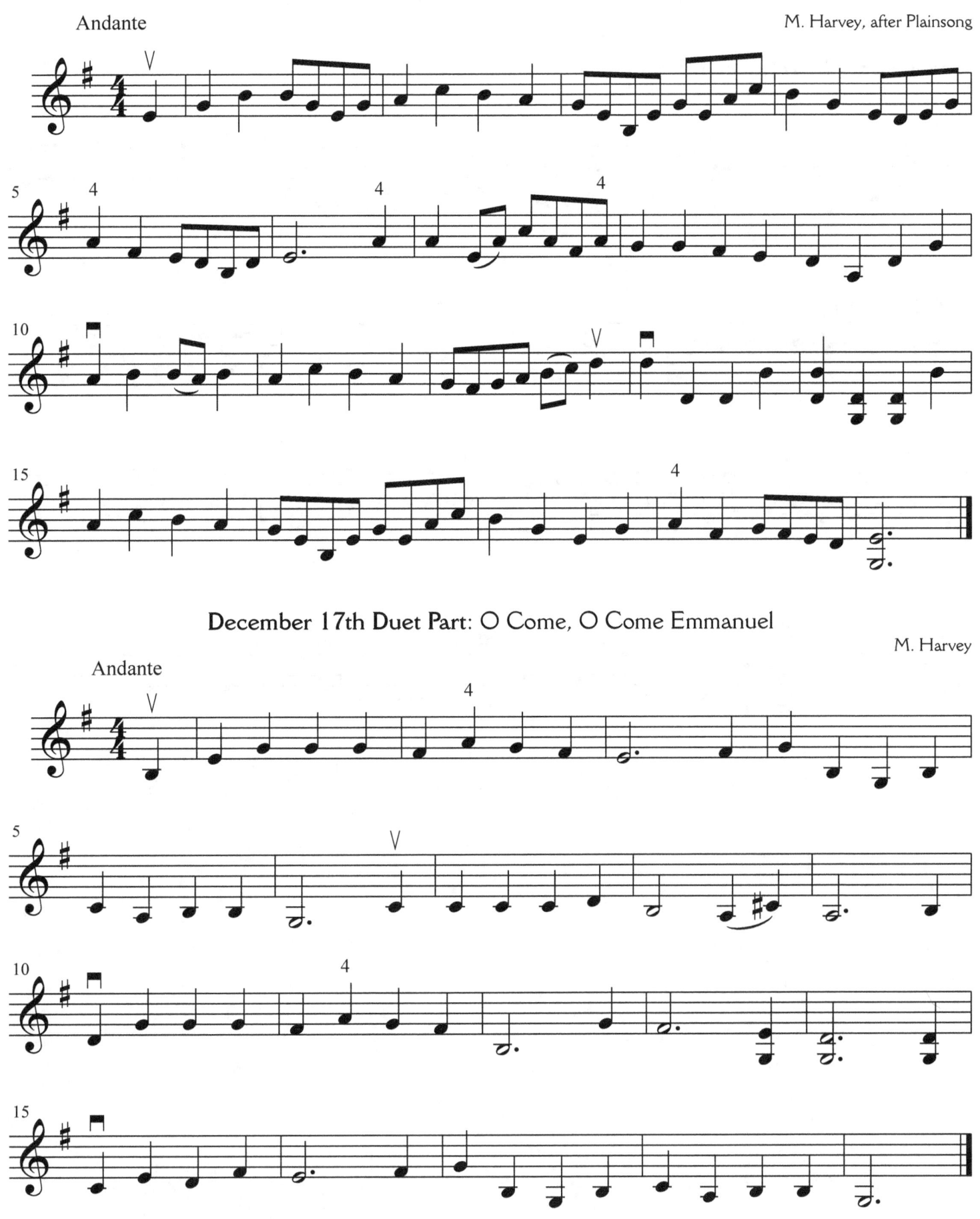

©2022 C. Harvey Publications All Rights Reserved.

December 18th: Warm-Ups for The Twelve Days of Christmas

Twelve Days Bow Rhythm Etude

C. Harvey

Twelve Days Agililty Etude

C. Harvey

December 18th Melody: The Twelve Days of Christmas

Allegro   Traditional Melody

December 18th Variation: The Twelve Days of Christmas

Allegro   M. Harvey, after Traditional Melody

©2022 C. Harvey Publications All Rights Reserved.

December 18th Duet Part: The Twelve Days of Christmas

M. Harvey

December 19th: Warm-Up for Carol of the Bells

C. Harvey

December 19th Melody: Carol of the Bells

M. Leontovych

Allegro

©2022 C. Harvey Publications All Rights Reserved.

December 20th: Warm-Up for Deck the Halls

C. Harvey

December 20th Melody: Deck the Halls

T. Oliphant

Allegro

December 21st: Warm-Up for Hark, the Herald Angels Sing

C. Harvey

December 21st Melody: Hark, the Herald Angels Sing

F. Mendelssohn

Moderato

December 21st Variation: Hark, the Herald Angels Sing

M. Harvey, after F. Mendelssohn

December 21st Duet Part: Hark, the Herald Angels Sing

M. Harvey

December 22nd: Warm-Ups for Waltz from *The Nutcracker*

G♯ Study

C. Harvey

E♯ Study

C. Harvey

Scale Rhythm Study

C. Harvey

December 22nd Melody: Waltz of the Flowers, from *The Nutcracker*

P. Tchaikovsky

Tempo di Valse

December 22nd Variation: Waltz of the Flowers, from *The Nutcracker*

P. Tchaikovsky, arr. M. Harvey

Tempo di Valse

©2022 C. Harvey Publications All Rights Reserved.

December 22nd Duet Part: Waltz of the Flowers, from *The Nutcracker*

M. Harvey, after P. Tchaikovsky

Tempo di Valse

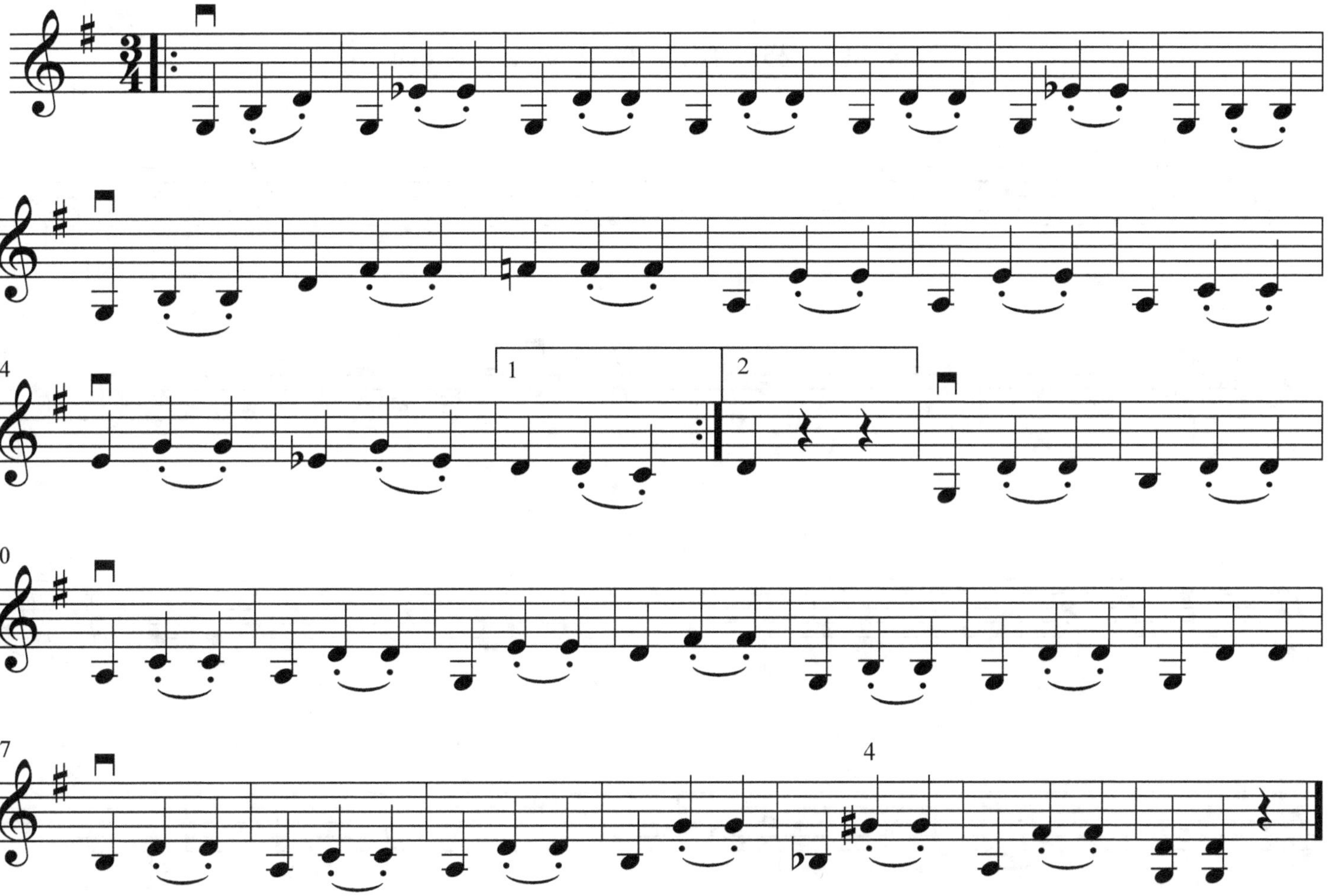

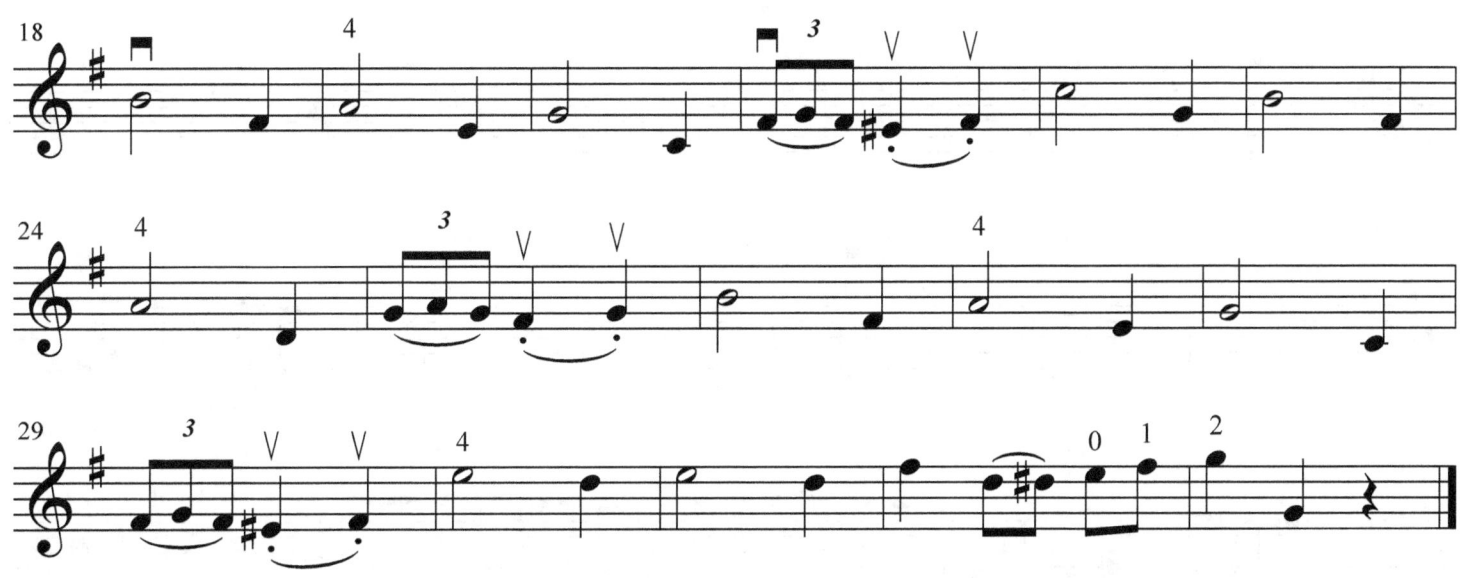

December 25th: Warm-Up for We Wish You a Merry Christmas

C. Harvey

December 25th Melody: We Wish You a Merry Christmas

Vivace

Traditional Melody

A Violin Advent, Book One

December 25th Variation: We Wish You a Merry Christmas

M. Harvey, after Traditional Melody

December 25th Duet Part: We Wish You a Merry Christmas

M. Harvey

©2022 C. Harvey Publications All Rights Reserved.

Available from www.charveypublications.com
The Blackberry Blossom Fiddle Book for Violin

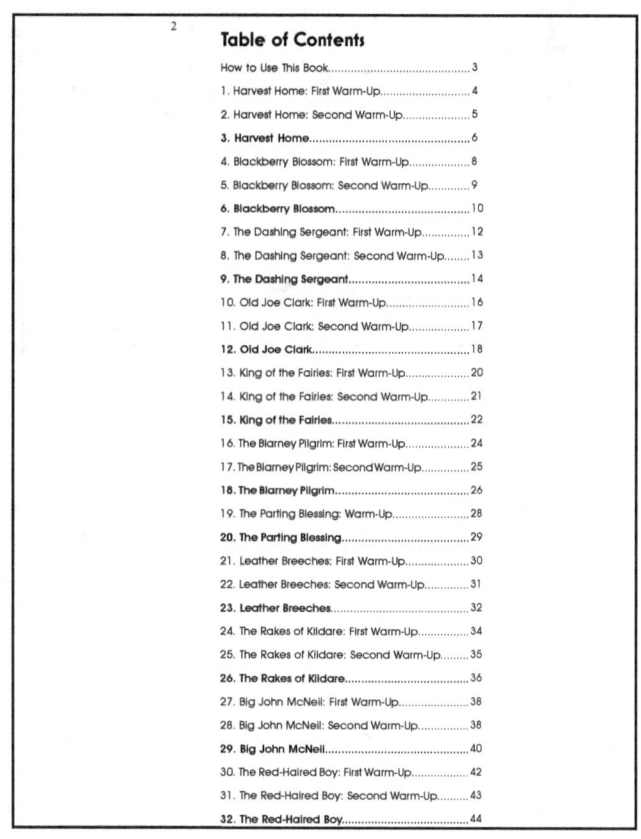

Fiddle Exercises at two different levels.

Fiddle Tunes at two different levels can be played solo, in duets, or in chamber ensembles.

Exercises, Tunes, and Harmonies are compatible with the viola, cello, and string bass books!

www.ingramcontent.com/pod-product-compliance
Lightning Source LLC
Chambersburg PA
CBHW081406070526
44583CB00020B/2705